Water Baptism

By Harold H. Milton

© 2016 Janice Louise Blanton

All rights reserved. No part of this publication may be reproduced or transmitted in any form or by any means electronic or mechanical, including photocopy, recording, or any information storage and retrieval system, without permission in writing from the copyright owner.

Requests for permission to make copies of any part of this work should be mailed to:

Janice L. Blanton
376 Canterbury Road
Bay Village, Ohio 44140

ISBN: 978-1-62550 277-3

1-62550-277-X

Printed in the United States of America

Harold H. Milton, died in 1998. He was born in 1913.
It is therefore that I, Janice L. Blanton, speak for my Dad
to complete his dreams. Harold was generous to those
who were down on their luck and life's obligations
that prevented him from the publishing of his writings of 40 years.
I, Janice, dedicate to my mother, Nellie Agnes Romeo Blanton, 1924-
1960, my father Orville, 1922-1960, Harold's wife, Jane,
his daughter, Nancy, 1950-1970 ,his parents, Eva, 1885-1963,
Charles, 1872-1946, grandfather Marion, 1845-1920,
fought in the civil war his siblings, Hazel, Myrtle, Jewell, and Mary,
my dear friend, Robert F Burkhardt, and
the Church of Christ and to myself, Janice Louise Blanton.

Acknowledgement

Harold H. Milton's first book Mountain Dew was completed after twelve years while he was writing other novels and short stories. He began his ideas in the 1930s. He was German and born in Marietta, Ohio December 23 rd. 1913 ,the only red haired son of Charles Henry Milton born February 10th. 1872 and whom passed away November 22, 1946 and Eva Marilla Farley born January 6th. 1885 and passing away April 1963. He had three older Sisters named Hazel, Myrtle, Jewell and one younger named Mary. They lived in a small cabin and had their education in a one room school house. Their poverty was severe and Harold was embarrassed to carry all five lunches to school in a basket. During the Depression Harold had to quit school in the eighth grade to help his Father with farming and hunt Ginseng and yellowroot for profit. Together they traveled for many days throughout the vast woods of West Virginia. There were many attempts to move there as they had pushed a covered wagon but the wheels would get stuck in mud or the wagon broke down.. Harold loved these times with his Father and they would have contests to see who would find the most herbs. Harold moved to Cleveland, Ohio in his twentys and married Jane A. Romeo from West Virginia. Jane was born October 3rd. 1925 of Dutch, Italian and English decent. He worked for White Motors. She passed away December 1986.

It was a cold blizzardy day when 1- Janice Louise Blanton was born in Cleveland, Ohio on January 16th., 1955 to Nellie Agnes Romeo who was born February 1st. 1924 in Gypsy, West Virginia and Orville B. Blanton born July 18th. 1922 in Kentucky. The rule at Booth Memorial- a Salvation Army Hospital for unwed Mothers was that You could live there your last trimester ,you had to do chores and you had to relinquish your baby. Nellie took me home and my first crib was a dresser drawer for five months. She then married Orville and continued her waitress job while Harold and Jane babysat me from four months on. Five years later my Mother Nellie died of Leukemia at 36 years young and Harold agreed to raise me full time while my Father Orville visited often until he died in 1966 at 43 years old of heart disease.

In 1960 Harold knocked on many doors and built a congregation to open a Church of Christ. We spent weekends walking thru the woods collecting ginseng that dried out in our attic and was sold. He loved to talk about his childhood days and speak German with his Daughter Nancy who also died at nineteen years old of a brain tumor while in her second year of Cleveland State University. She was a lovely redhead and we loved each other as Sisters and laughed a lot and played tennis. The feeling of my being orphaned kept getting worse but Harold was there for me and it made us closer to be Father and Daughter. As children Nancy and I were asked by him "what do you girls want when my books hit it big?" Her answer was a white baby grand piano.

For forty years he wrote and typed books that were wanted for publishing in New York, he never had the finances for this and Nancy's college loans and funeral expenses were high, though he continued writing.

With my encouragement he completed his G.E.D. at 79 years old. I had a nice party and it made the newspaper and he planned to go to College but we moved to a different home further away. He always wanted to see the Grand Canyon so in 1994 we went there. We stayed in Vegas he liked that also and would imitate a robot dancing that he had seen in a show. He died at eighty four years old as I held his hand in the hospital. I had saved his life over thirty times when he had chest pain, I was now a emergency room Registered Nurse working all departments however up to 100 hours a week. As I watched Harolds passing I was saddened that his departing was such a *loss*, for he knew his Bible word for word and was so nice, kind and smart. I inspired to become a Nurse at age eight and had taken care of him when he was very sick before and after a surgery in 1963. He had taken care of me also. Around 2000 I noticed his books under my stairwell and read some of it, however in 2013 I wanted to get them published and leave his fingerprint in the world.

It is now through my labor of love that I present to you the writings of my second Father Harold Homer Milton. As I now carry out his dream and pull back the curtain of time and the past he smiles down from heaven and becomes a known author. I can now sit back and listen to Nancy play on her white baby grand piano. His five books are named Mountain *Dew,* The Treasure of the Hills, Water Baptism, The Conquest of Lonnie Dolan and The Appalacian Collection: Remembering the Hill Country.

Fondly and with great honor,
Janice Louise Blanton

Introduction

The importance of water baptism in Christ's plan for human redemption has been a subject of many long and varied discussions. There are those who are taught that water baptism has no part in our salvation. That to have faith in the Lord Jesus is all that is necessary. The New Testament[1] sets forth very plainly that we must do *more* than believe in the Lord Jesus if we are to be found acceptable to him. The Son of God only commends in part those who look to him for salvation.

In the following pages, you will become acquainted with the biblical history of water baptism. I will discuss this ordinance's first appearance in the New Testament, and then follow it through the lives of John the Baptist and Jesus Christ, and the teachings of the apostles after Jesus ascended back to the Father.

---

[1] Throughout this book, I will reference and recount passages from the King James Version of the Bible.

Harold H. Milton

I will furnish undisputable scriptural proof that being baptized with water is a command of the Lord Jesus. And we must obey this command if we hope to enter into the kingdom of heaven.

John the Baptist was given to the world before the Lord Jesus to prepare the way for him. John the Baptist was sent to establish water baptism. In the following pages, you will see that John the Baptist baptized Jesus in the river Jordan.

In Saint John 3:1-15, Nicodemus the Pharisee visited Jesus at nighttime. The Saviour was very emphatic in his answer to Nicodemus's question. The following pages will prove to you that the answer Jesus gave to Nicodemus applies to every person, to every nation under the sun, as long as time shall last.

You will see in the following pages that Jesus, just before his ascension, gave his disciples instructions to preach the gospel. To every creature.[2] He wanted them baptized in the name of the Father, the Son, and the Holy Ghost.[3]

How well his disciples carried out his final instructions is addressed in the following pages.

---

[2] Mark 16:15.
[3] Matthew 28:19.

Water Baptism

Many of you may contend that the Apostle Paul teaches that baptism is not essential to our salvation. This is not the case. The scriptural record shows this. Paul himself was baptized in the city of Damascus, and he was called to preach the gospel of Christ Jesus. And water baptism has a definite place in that gospel.

It is my earnest desire to prove to you that we are under command by the Lord Jesus to observe baptism. That is my sole purpose for writing.

Chapter 1

The Birth of John the Baptist

Water baptism made its first appearance in the New Testament. The term *baptism*[4] means "a ceremonial immersion in water, or application of water, as an initiatory rite or sacrament of the Christian church." *To baptize* means "to plunge into"; "place under a liquid"; "to sink"; "to bury." Thus we can clearly see that to be baptized with water means to be immersed or buried in water, or, in other words, *to be buried in baptism*. Like it says in Colossians 2:12: "Buried with him [Jesus] in baptism, wherein also ye are risen with *him* through the faith of the operation of God, who hath raised him from the dead."

This ordinance was brought into practice by John the Baptist as a means of washing away sins. So you may get a better understanding of how the ordinance of water baptism came into practice, I am

---

[4] Random House Kernerman Webster's College Dictionary.

going to recount for you the birth and childhood of John the Baptist as it appears in Saint Luke 1:5-25.

More than two thousand years ago there ruled over Judaea a king whose name was Herod. At this same time there was in the country of Judaea a priest named Zacharias. He had a wife, Elizabeth, and she was a descendant of the daughters of Aaron. Zacharias and his wife were just people. They followed all the commandments and ordinances that God had given to them, in a manner that was most pleasing to the Lord. Nevertheless, these good people were childless because Elizabeth was barren. They were both quite old, though, and in the latter days of their natural lives.

One day as Zacharias went to perform his priestly duty of burning incense, which he was obligated to do as soon as he entered the Lord's temple, he saw that an angel of the lord was standing on the right of the altar of incense. And outside the temple, the people who were righteous were praying and waiting for Zacharias to burn the incense. When Zacharias saw the angel, he was very much afraid. But the angel told him not to be frightened. His appearance was in answer to Zacharias's prayers for a child. Then the angel told Zacharias that his wife, Elizabeth, would bear him a son, and that he was to name this son John.

Water Baptism

And then the angel told Zacharias that his son's birth would cause the people to rejoice. For his son would be great in the Lord's eyes. He would not drink strong spirits or wine, and he would be filled with the Holy Ghost while still inside his mother. Later, he would turn many of the unrighteous of Israel to the ways of the Lord their God.

As is the case today, many were following only their own lusts and desires. More than the Lord God wanted them to. Wrapped up in their own egotistical ways, the children of Israel were leading lives that were displeasing to God.

The Lord God that the angel was referring to was none other than Christ Jesus. The angel told Zacharias that the son that was going to be born to him and his wife, Elizabeth, had been ordained by God Almighty to come to this earth before the Son of God, who would follow in the wake of Zacharias's son John. Ordained to go before Christ, in the spirit and power of Elias, John would turn the hearts of the people away from their disobedience. He would also turn the parents' hearts back to their children's well-beings, and he would prepare the people of Israel for the gospel of Christ that would follow John's ministry.

When Zacharias heard these things that the angel was saying about this son that was going to be born to him and his wife, he was unbelieving. He asked the angel for a sign so he would know for sure these things would happen. He was an old man, after all, and Elizabeth, his wife, was also old, well past childbearing years. These things of which the angel was telling him were unthinkable to Zacharias. To have a son at this time in his life was beyond his understanding. Something of this sort was the direct reverse of all the laws of nature. Zacharias had not stopped to realize that this message had come to him from the most High God, with whom nothing is impossible.

The angel was angry at Zacharias for his unbelief. He told Zacharias his name was Gabriel, and that he stood always in the presence of God, who had sent him to Zacharias to tell him of his coming good fortune. As penalty for his unbelief, the angel struck Zacharias dumb and took away his ability to speak, until the day that Gabriel's words had come true.

Outside the temple, the people were wondering why Zacharias was taking so long to perform his priestly duties. When he finally emerged, they knew that he must have seen a vision in the temple for he could no longer speak. He made signs with his hands to communicate as such. Gabriel's penalty would last until Zacharias's child was named.

Now, after certain days had passed, Elizabeth conceived. Shortly after, she went into seclusion for a period of five months. Elizabeth was happy, for God had looked at her and enabled her to conceive, taking away the contempt people had shown her for being childless.

Now, dear reader, I am going to pause here a moment in my account of the birth of John the Baptist. You see, the story of his birth, to parents that were old and stricken in years, has a parallel in biblical history. At the very beginning of the Israelite people, Abram and his wife, Sarai, like Zacharias and Elizabeth, had a son later in life. Their story figures largely in ten chapters of the book of Genesis in the Old Testament.

The first time the Lord God speaks to Abram about his "seed" is in Genesis 12:7. He speaks of giving land to Abram's descendants, which Abram does not have at the time.

When the Lord first called Abram he was seventy-five years old and his wife, Sarai, was sixty-five. In Genesis 17:5, the Lord changes Abram's name to Abraham. In Genesis 17:15, he changes Sarai's name to Sarah. The record shows that many years passed before the promised son was born. To be exact, the time that passed was twenty-five years. During this time, the Lord kept renewing his promise of a son to the elderly couple. Eventually, Abraham and his wife, Sarah, scoffed at the thought of becoming parents. Genesis 17:16-17 says that Abraham fell on his face during one of the Lord's visits after the Lord told Abraham that he would bless Sarah with a son. Abraham laughed for he did not believe it was possible. He was a hundred years old and Sarah was ninety.

In Genesis 18:1-15, the Lord appeared to Abraham again. He sent three messengers to Abraham, who, at the time, was dwelling in the plains of Mamre. These messengers from God told Abraham that the Lord would visit when the time was right, and his wife would conceive and bring forth a son. Sarah heard these words and laughed in her heart. She and her husband were old, and the weight of age sat heavily on their shoulders. And Sarah had long since passed that time in her life when she could hope to become a mother. She was barren, always had been. That was why she laughed when she heard the words of the messengers.

The Lord was wroth with this elderly couple for their unbelief. He asked Abraham why his wife had laughed. Did she think that anything was too difficult for the Lord? Sarah denied that she had laughed, because she was afraid. But the messengers rebuked her for her denial, telling her that she did laugh. Unlike Zacharias, neither Abraham nor Sarah were punished for their unbelief. And in Genesis 21:1-5 the Lord fulfilled his promise to Abraham and Sarah, and Sarah conceived and bore a son, whom they named Isaac.

Read the biblical story of this miraculous birth. It shows that if we trust in God, he will bless us in wondrous ways. But first we must obey his commands, and the commands of his son. And we are under command by the Lord Jesus to observe baptism. I will resume, now, the account of John the Baptist's birth, picking up where I left off with my recounting of Saint Luke 1:26-35.

In the sixth month of Elizabeth's pregnancy, the Lord sent the angel Gabriel on another mission. This time the angel was sent to the wife of Joseph, whose name was Mary, who dwelled in the city of Nazareth, of Galilee. Gabriel greeted Mary with the words that she was highly favored, the Lord being pleased with her, and she was blessed among women. Mary was mystified at the manner of Gabriel's greeting. She wondered what he could mean. Gabriel told Mary to fear not, because she had found favor in the eyes of God. Therefore she would conceive in her womb and bring forth a son that she was to call Jesus. This son, the angel told her, would be great, and he would be known as the Son of the Highest. He would be given, by his father, the Lord God, the throne of his earthly father David. He would reign over the house of Israel forever. And his kingdom would be everlasting.

When Mary heard the words of Gabriel, she was astonished. She was still a virgin, having had, as yet, no sexual relations with her husband, Joseph. Then Gabriel informed Mary that the Holy Ghost would come upon her, and the power of the Highest would overshadow her. And the holy child that she would bare would be known as the Son of God.

Here again we see the limitless power of God. In this case, we see Christ Jesus coming from the Father in heaven and entering into the womb of the Virgin Mary, to be born in the natural way. In the case of Elizabeth and Sarah, the Lord had to perform two wondrous miracles to bring about the births of their sons. They were both old, so the Lord had to rejuvenate their aged bodies, and then, upon sexual relations with their husbands, they became pregnant. But for Mary, the Lord God brought about her pregnancy through his wondrous power. He placed Christ Jesus in her womb.

This child was the Messiah that was to come. The Son of God. He would come down from the mansions of heaven to take upon himself the form of sinful flesh, to dwell on this earth as one of us,

Water Baptism

having and overcoming the same trials and temptations that beset every human being. Christ would follow in the path that John the Baptist would prepare for him. He would come to establish his kingdom, to grant salvation to all who accepted his gospel. Christ was coming to give the human family a new plan for human redemption.

Let us pick up the recounting with Saint Luke 1:36-80. Mary resigned herself to the will of God, and the angel withdrew from her presence. Shortly after this had come to pass, she rose and went to visit her cousin Elizabeth, Zacharias's wife. The angel Gabriel had told Mary of Elizabeth's pregnancy; therefore, aside from the fact that they were related, they had much in common. Both had received visits from the angel Gabriel, who had told them of their coming motherhood. And both had been told beforehand what their unborn sons were to be named. Thus it is easy to see how they would have much to talk about together.

Mary and Elizabeth praised God for being chosen as the women to give birth to the Christ child and John the Baptist. This was, indeed, a great honor. Mary has been praised down through the centuries as the mother of Jesus. Elizabeth has not enjoyed the same distinction that Mary has, but she gave birth to a great man, too. A man who was chosen to pave the way for the Lord Jesus, who was chosen to lay the *foundation* for the gospel of Christ. He was sent by God the Father to institute baptism. To preach "the baptism of repentance for the remission of sins."[5] This was the man that Elizabeth, the barren one, gave birth to.

Mary was with her cousin Elizabeth for about three months, and then she returned to her own home in Nazareth, of Galilee. In the due course of time, the wife of Zacharias brought forth a son. On the eighth day after his birth, the relatives and neighbors of these good people came and circumcised the child, and they named him Zacharias, after his father. But his mother, Elizabeth, informed those who were gathered in their home that the child was to be named John. They told her that none of the kinfolk bore that name. But she was insistent. Then the people asked Zacharias what he would call his son.

Saint Luke 1:63 tells us that Zacharias asked for a writing tablet and wrote: "His name is John." And all those that saw what he had written stared with wonder.

As you will recall, the angel Gabriel had made Zacharias dumb, rendering him speechless. It was his penalty for his unbelief that his

---

[5] Luke 3:3.

wife, Elizabeth, would bear him a son. That dumbness, Gabriel told him, would continue until Zacharias's son was born and named.

When Zacharias wrote that his son was to be named John, his tongue was loosed and he was able to speak once more. And he immediately began to praise God. Zacharias then prophesied and gave praises unto the Lord God of Israel, giving thanks that God had not forgotten his people of Israel. Zacharias continued at great length, setting forth all the blessings that would be visited upon the children of Israel through this child John that was born to them. He set forth that his son would be known as the prophet of the Highest, and he would go before the Lord Jesus to prepare the people for his coming.

John would give knowledge of salvation to the people of Israel, giving light to those who were sitting in the darkness of sin and in the shadow of death. This child was destined to guide the feet of the people of Israel onto paths of peace.

The scriptures tell us that John the Baptist grew and waxed strong in spirit. This son of Zacharias was unusual. He was a dweller of desert places, until that day when he would be called forth by the voice of God to preach to the people of Israel. He lived a secluded life and lived off the land, eating locusts and wild honey, and clothing himself with the skins of animals.

When you stop to consider this man, John the Baptist, you will see that he truly was a prophet sent from God, in every sense of the word. His birth was miraculous, and his childhood and early life in the wilderness were lived in total obscurity. This man was prepared for this mission by God Almighty. He had no educational instruction of any sort. Yet when the time came for him to bring the Lord Jesus's message to the people, he began preaching and baptizing with no hesitation whatsoever. He was answering the call of duty for the gospel of Christ for which he was born into this world.

When next we read of John the Baptist, he will have begun his ministry.

Chapter 2

The Birth of Jesus Christ

I have recounted for you the story of how the Lord sent the angel Gabriel to Mary in the city of Nazareth, and how Gabriel informed her that she would bring forth a son who was to be named Jesus, who would be known as the Son of the Highest. Mary, a virgin, became with child through the power of Almighty God.

Now, in the following pages, I will tell you how Christ was born in Bethlehem. I will tell you about the manner of his lowly birth, his circumcision, and his early childhood. In order to give you a complete picture of Christ's early years, I will recount only portions of three chapters from the New Testament. I will begin with Saint Matthew 1:18-25.

When Joseph, the husband of Mary, found that she was with child, he was much troubled. For as yet, he had not known Mary truly as a wife. But being a fair man, he contemplated hiding her away secretly, rather than making a public example of her. While he was mediating on this matter, an angel of the Lord appeared to him in a dream. The angel told him not to fear accepting Mary as his wife. The power of the Holy Ghost had made her with child. Then the angel told him that the child would be a son, and his name was to be Jesus. And he would save his people from their sins.

Joseph woke and did as the angel requested. He accepted Mary as his wife, but he did not know her intimately until after she had delivered her firstborn son.

Now, there are certain facts surrounding the birth of the child Jesus that I want you to know. These facts are from Saint Luke 2:1-20.

When Mary was far advanced in her pregnancy, there went out an order from the Roman emperor, Caesar Augustus, that all the world was going to be taxed. The Roman empire had, through conquest, gained control of the civilized world. This had happened approximately twenty-seven years prior to the time Jesus was born on this earth. As is the case when a government exists, it operates on the taxes that are collected from the people it represents. And since the Roman government controlled the civilized world of that day, the people of Israel were subject to Roman taxation.

So we find Joseph and Mary being compelled to respond to the order that Cesar sent out. Every person, according to the rules set forth, had to report to his own city to be taxed. Joseph was of the house and lineage of David; therefore, he and his wife, Mary, left their home in Nazareth and traveled to the country of Judaea, to the city of David, which was known as Bethlehem.

As I mentioned earlier, Mary was far advanced in her pregnancy. And while they were there in Bethlehem, she told her husband that it was time for her child to be born. She delivered her firstborn son, swaddled him in blankets, and then laid him in a manger.

A quick interruption here, dear reader, I want to point out that a *manger* is a boxlike trough that cattle and horses eat out of. Such was the first bed that our Saviour had upon this earth. Why?

Because there was no room for them in the inns of Bethlehem.

This housing shortage was doubtless due to the order of taxation that had gone out to the people. Aside from that, the innkeepers had no consideration for these weary travelers. They did not care that Mary was great with child. If they had cared, our Saviour would not have been born in a shelter for the beasts of the fields.

That is how Jesus made his entrance into this world. A world that received him not. A world that he had come to save, nevertheless.

The night that Jesus was born, there were shepherds keeping watch over their flocks in the fields outside the city of Bethlehem. And an angel of the Lord appeared to them. The scriptures tell us that the glory of the Lord shone around them and the shepherds were much afraid. But the angel was the bearer of good tidings and told the shepherds to not be afraid. The good tidings, the angel said that night, were for the whole world. For all the people of every nation, everywhere. For that day, the angel told the shepherds, in the city of David, which is Bethlehem, a Saviour was born, which was Christ the Lord.

Then suddenly the angel was not alone. For there appeared with the angel a vast assembly of the heavenly host, praising God: "Glory to God in the highest, and on this earth peace, and goodwill toward men."[6]

What a beautiful benediction. Peace on earth. *Peace* is something that this old world has never known. Mankind, I am sad

---

[6] Luke 2:14.

to relate, has little goodwill toward one another. The reason for this sad condition is Satan, the deceiver of mankind.

After the angels had disappeared, the shepherds journeyed with haste into Bethlehem to see the Saviour that had been born. They found Joseph and Mary, and the baby Jesus lying in a manger, just as the angel had foretold they would. The shepherds spread the word abroad about the Christ child.

I will tell you what it says in Saint Luke later in this chapter. But now, I want to tell you what Saint Matthew 2:1-12 says.

Wise men came from the east to inquire about the one who was born to be king of the Jews, for they had seen his star, and they had come to worship him.

Now, when Herod, the king who ruled over the people of Israel at that time, heard these things about Jesus, he was greatly disturbed, and all those of Jerusalem were troubled with him. He left no stone unturned in his efforts to learn where Jesus was born. He questioned the wise men about the time the star appeared. He gathered the chief priests and scribes and asked them where this prophesied king was to be born. And they told him, according to the writings of the prophet, Christ was going to be born in Bethlehem.

Herod then called the wise men to him and sent them to Bethlehem to find the child Jesus, and when they had found him, he told them, he wanted them to send word back because he wished to come and worship the Lord Jesus too.

The star went before the wise men and guided them to the place where the child was. When the star reached this place, it remained stationary over it. The wise men did not return to Herod with any information, nor did they send anyone in their stead. God had warned them in a dream not to return to Herod, for Herod had no thought in his heart about worshipping this Jewish king that was born in Bethlehem. When he heard that this child was born king of the Jewish people, he reasoned that his kingdom was going to be taken from him. Therefore, his intentions were to find Jesus and kill him. But that did not happen. The wise men took precautions. They traveled a different route home than the one they had come to Bethlehem by so as to avoid giving the child's location away to Herod and his people.

The description of these wise men of long ago worshipping the baby Jesus has been handed down through the centuries. Saint Matthew 2:11 says that when they came to where Jesus was, they fell to their knees before him and worshipped him. Then they opened their treasures and gave him gifts of gold, and myrrh, and frankincense.[7]

Saint Matthew 2:13-14 explain what happened after the wise men left the baby Jesus.

Joseph, like the wise men, was warned in a dream by an angel of God to flee to Egypt with the child Jesus and his mother, and to remain there until the Lord informed him that it was safe to return to his homeland. Because Herod was going to search for the baby Jesus to do away with him. When Joseph woke, he gathered the baby and his mother, and fled into Egypt under cover of the night.

Let us pause for a moment and consider the hostile way our Saviour was received into this world. He was born in a shelter for the beasts of the fields, because the innkeepers turned Joseph and Mary away to find shelter as best they could. Then when Jesus was but a few days or weeks old, Joseph spirited him and his mother off to Egypt to escape the diabolical scheme that Herod had invented for the purpose of slaying the Christ child.

---

[7] *Frankincense* is a fragrant gum resin obtained from various burseraceous trees, chiefly of East Africa. This is an important incense resin.

You see, in Saint Matthew 2:16-18, when Herod learned that the wise men had not followed his instructions, but had mocked him, he was furious. Whereupon, he then revealed his true intentions regarding his interest in the baby. He issued an order to have all the boys under the age of two in Bethlehem killed. Thus Herod reasoned that by this action he would surely slay the child that had been born king of the Jews.

But the little child Jesus was safely out of his reach. He was in Egypt.

Saint Matthew 2:19-23 say that Joseph remained in Egypt with his little family until an angel of the Lord informed him in a dream that Herod was dead, and that it was safe to return to the land of Israel. Joseph woke and bid his wife, Mary, to ready herself and the child Jesus, for they were returning to the land from which they had fled.

But the son of Herod, Archelaus, had succeeded to the throne on his father's death, and when Joseph heard this, he was afraid. Doubtless Joseph believed that Archelaus might attempt to slay the child Jesus, as his father had sought to do.

So, upon a warning received from God in a dream, Joseph and his little family changed direction and headed to the city of

Water Baptism

Nazareth. The same city that he and his wife, Mary, had formerly dwelt in.

Joseph's flight into Egypt and his eventual residence in Nazareth were foretold by the prophets. It was prophesied that the Lord would call his Son out of Egypt, and Jesus, according to the prophets, would be called a Nazarene. Jesus lived in Nazareth until he was thirty years old. At which time he began his ministry.

Now, Saint Luke 2:21-24 tell us that before their flight to Egypt, Joseph and Mary took the child Jesus to Jerusalem to present him to the Lord. This was done in observance of an ancient law of the Lord. Joseph and Mary offered the proper sacrifice required for this occasion.

I will recount, now, the encounters they had with Simeon, a devout man, and Anna, a prophetess, as laid out in Saint Luke 2:25-38.

There lived in Jerusalem a devout man whose name was Simeon. He was led by the Spirit of God to the temple on the same day that Joseph and Mary brought the child Jesus to observe the custom of the law. The Holy Ghost had promised this man that death would not overtake him until he had seen the Christ child. When Simeon saw Mary with the baby, he took the baby Jesus in his arms and praised God. He said to the Lord that he could now die in peace as the Lord had promised, for his eyes had beheld the salvation that the Lord had promised would come to this world. The light of the world. Simeon blessed Joseph and Mary. And he told them that this child of theirs would be responsible for the fall, and rising again, of many of the people of Israel.

A prophetess of great age named Anna, who faithfully visited the temple to serve God, came in at the moment Simeon was blessing Joseph and Mary. She, like Simeon, gave thanks to the Lord for this happy occasion. She spoke of the Christ child to all those of Jerusalem who looked for redemption. This baby son was the promised Redeemer. The Messiah. The Son of God. The people of Israel had looked forward to his coming for many centuries.

The record that Saint Luke gives, concerning this early part of Christ's life on this earth, tells us that after Joseph and Mary had performed all the required things at the temple for this occasion, according to the law of the Lord, they returned to their home in Nazareth.[8] Saint Luke does not mention their flight into Egypt to escape the destructive intentions of Herod. Only Saint Matthew

---

[8] Luke 2:39.

recorded their flight.[9] Both, however, agree that at some point after the birth of Jesus, Joseph and Mary returned to Nazareth with him. And there, in Nazareth, Jesus lived with his parents until the day when he began his ministry.

I am going to recount for you, now, something that happened when Jesus was twelve years old. Saint Luke 2:41-52 tell us that the people of Israel celebrated the Passover every year with a feast. This feast, even today, commemorates the passing of the destroying angel over the houses of the Israelites when he slew the firstborns of the Egyptians. This act freed the Israelites from the Egyptians' slavery.

Every year, Joseph and Mary would go to Jerusalem to celebrate the Passover feast. When Jesus was twelve years old, he went with them to Jerusalem to celebrate this feast. And when the days of the feast were completed, they started their journey back to Nazareth. But Jesus was not in the group that journeyed back. He remained behind in Jerusalem. Joseph and Mary were not aware of this. They thought he was mixed in with the relatives and acquaintances they were traveling homeward with, probably playing with the other children. A day's march was behind them before they sought him

---

[9] Matthew 2:13-15.

out. He was only twelve years old, after all, and they wanted to make sure he was all right.

They searched the group for him without success, so they turned back to Jerusalem. After three days of anxious searching, they finally found their son in the temple. He was sitting with the learned men of the day, listening intently to what they had to say and asking them intelligent questions. Those who heard him were astounded at his understanding of the subjects the men spoke of.

When we stop to consider a moment, we are confronted by this fact: Jesus was reigning in glory with the Father for innumerable ages before this world was ever created. Therefore, when he came to this earth to dwell with us, as one of us, he was possessed with a wisdom and understanding that was far, *far* beyond the ordinary human's. Jesus helped the Father create this earth. So he knew all about this earth and the people who live on it from the very first. Knowing this, we can understand and share the astonishment that those who heard him that day must have felt.

When his parents saw him sitting among those learned men, they were much surprised. His mother asked him why he had done this to them. They had searched for him with heavy hearts.

Water Baptism

Imagine their anxiety. They had searched three days for him. Three days can seem like three years to parents at such a time.

Jesus was surprised that they had looked for him. He asked them, "How is it that ye sought me? Wist ye not that I must be about my Father's business?"[10]

Even at the early age of twelve, Jesus was answering the call of duty. He wondered why his earthly parents had bothered to look for him when they had found him missing on the way back to Nazareth. He had come to this earth to bring the will of God, his Father, to his people. Therefore, he asked them a straightforward question: Know you not that I must be about my Father's business? He knew what his mission on this earth was for. Christ was endowed with an age-old wisdom. A wisdom that was given to him in glory, before this world ever existed.[11]

On that day in Jerusalem, the Lord Jesus was but a mere lad. But he was not an ordinary one. This boy was the Son of God. And he was sent to this earth to save that which was lost, and that is what he was doing. He was laying down his plan for our salvation; he was gathering information to save our human souls. Doubtless he felt

---

[10] Luke 2:49.
[11] John 17:5.

that the time to harvest the information he needed was short, as human life is so fleeting.

His parents were not able to understand his attitude toward their anxiety for his welfare that day. But his mother kept all these things that Jesus had spoken to them in her heart. She knew that she had brought a son into this world that she would not be able to understand. The angel Gabriel had told her that the child that she would give birth to would be the Son of God. And that day Mary was seeing this fact brought home to her.

Jesus returned to Nazareth with his parents and began to obey them as an ordinary son would. Saint Luke 2:52 tells us that he increased in wisdom and grew to be a man, and that he was well liked by the people. All the while, his favor with God, his Father, increased.

Now, as I have said, Jesus was twelve years old when he was found in the temple sitting with the learned men of the time. From that time until he was baptized by John the Baptist, eighteen years passed without being recorded.

One of the great unanswered questions is this: What happened in the life of Christ during those eighteen years?

Water Baptism

Saint Matthew 13:55 only tells us that he was the son of Joseph, the carpenter. Therefore we must conclude that he worked at the carpenter trade with Joseph, his earthly father. The New Testament does not mention, in any way, anything about Jesus preaching or teaching the gospel during those years. Why? Because John the Baptist was sent to go before Christ to prepare the way for the gospel that was to follow. So the only correct explanation for why Jesus did not began his ministry sooner than he did was because he was waiting for the day John, the son of Zacharias, would come forth from his wilderness dwelling as John the Baptist. Then and only then, could Jesus begin his work as the Messiah, the one who would save his people and extend salvation to all nations, everywhere.

Christ and John the Baptist were very near the same earthly age, with John being six months the elder. As I have mentioned, their mothers were cousins,[12] but the scriptures say that John did not know Jesus when he baptized him.[13] This is proof of the seclusion that John the Baptist lived in before he began his ministry. It is unlikely that he even visited any of his relatives. If he had, he would

---

[12] Luke 1:36.
[13] John 1:33-34.

have known Jesus was his cousin. And he would have known that he was the Son of God, for the angel Gabriel had told Mary as such.[14]

In the next chapter John begins his ministry.

---

[14] Luke 1:26-38.

Chapter 3

Jesus is Baptized

There are four scriptural records of Jesus being baptized. One is given in each of the four gospels of the New Testament. Essentially, they are the same. Saint Matthew 3:1-17, however, gives the most complete record of Jesus being baptized by John. As such, that is the version I will recount for you here.

The call to his mission had come to John as he was dwelling in his wilderness home. And he responded to this call at once. He began preaching in the region of Judaea. He told the people to repent, for the kingdom of heaven was at hand. This John was the same man that was spoken of in biblical prophesy. His was the voice crying in the wilderness, preparing the way for the Lord Jesus. John's ministry heralded a new era. He was sent before Christ to establish water baptism as a means of washing away sins, no more would sins be washed away with blood.

By telling the people to repent, John was asking them to turn away from their sinful ways. And while telling them to do this, he was clothed in a most outlandish fashion. His garments were made of camel hair and he wore a leather girdle about his loins. These were the same garments that he wore in his wilderness home. His food was locusts and wild honey.

I cannot conceive in my mind any minister today preaching the gospel of Christ clothed in such fashion, or existing on such a diet. Can you? Truly, John the Baptist was a man apart, even in his day.

The people of Jerusalem and those that dwelt in Judaea and the entire region around the river Jordan came out to hear John. They confessed their sins to him and he baptized them in the river Jordan.

Many Pharisees and Sadducees came to where John was baptizing, and when he saw them, his greeting was in no uncertain terms friendly. He viewed these two Jewish sects as a generation of vipers, and he called them as such. Then he asked them who had warned them to change their ways, and thus escape the wrath of God that would eventually descend on the world.

Water Baptism

Let me pause here a moment to explain John's attitude. The Pharisees were a religious sect of the Jewish people at that time who stressed the exact observance of the law in an outward form. They observed the form, rather than the spirit, of the religion. In other words, the Pharisees were hypocrites.

Now the Sadducees were an ancient aristocratic Jewish group that held to the belief that there is no resurrection, or personal immortality to look forward to. Their doctrine was the teaching of free will.

It is no small wonder that John greeted these radicals as he did. Then he told them to bring forth fruits, or deeds, that would be worthy of repentance and baptism. And he warned them not to attempt to make excuses for themselves because Abraham was their forefather. John would have none of their attempts to shield their hypocrisy in this manner. Then he told them of a purge that was going to be conducted on the unfruitful, those who produced no good deeds.

John told them that he baptized with water, but the one that would come after him would baptize them with the Holy Ghost, and fire. This verse, Matthew 3:11, removes all argument to the effect that we must be baptized with water to obtain salvation. But let us look to the scriptures for the explanation of this statement that John made.

When a person is baptized with the Holy Ghost, the individual is not automatically exempt from water baptism. That person is still under command by Jesus Christ to be baptized with water. We need only to turn to the book of Acts for confirmation of this fact. In Acts 10:1-48, we find Simon Peter being sent for by Cornelius the Italian. Cornelius was a Gentile, and heretofore the gospel of Jesus Christ had only been preached to Jewish people. But Cornelius was a devout man who feared God, and an angel of God told him to send for Peter.

As Peter was preaching Christ to Cornelius and his household, the Holy Ghost fell on all who heard the word of God. Then Peter asked those who accompanied him from Joppa if any of them could forbid water, could forbid Cornelius and the other Gentiles present from being baptized, as they had received the Holy Ghost as well as the Jewish people. Then Peter commanded these people to be baptized in the name of the Lord.

Acts 11:1-18 tell us what happened next. When Simon Peter returned to the city of Jerusalem, he was accosted by those who had been circumcised. They had heard of his going to Cornelius, who

Water Baptism

was a Gentile and therefore uncircumcised, and of his eating with him. This was something that was strictly forbidden.

You see, the Jewish people were of the circumcision, which was a mark of distinction handed down from Abraham. It made them separate from all others and gave them first claim to salvation. So when Simon Peter went into the house of Cornelius and preached Jesus Christ to him and those that were gathered there, he was doing something that was unlawful for a Jew to do.

So that those who had accosted him would know exactly what had happened, Simon Peter told them everything, beginning with a vision he had had just before Cornelius's people arrived to get him. He recalled, too, the words that the Lord had spoken to him: "John indeed baptized with water; but ye shall be baptized with the Holy Ghost."[15] Peter went on to tell them that he could not stand against the will of God. After Peter told those who accosted him all this, they, too, accepted God's will.

In Saint Matthew 3:11-12, John the Baptist further states that Christ will separate the righteous from the unrighteous, and the unrighteous will be burned up with unquenchable fire.[16] John refers

---

[15] Acts 11:16.

[16] *Unquenchable fire* is fire that cannot be extinguished or put out.

to the righteous as "wheat," and the unrighteous as "chaff." This is similar to his previous statement in Saint Matthew 3:10 concerning the trees, meaning family trees, that do not bring forth good fruit, or good deeds. Such trees would be cut down and cast into the fire.

In Saint Matthew 3:11-12, John the Baptist considers himself unworthy to even unloose the latchets that fasten the shoes that the Lord Jesus wears. He knew that he had been sent before the Son of God to prepare the way. Nevertheless, he considered himself unworthy to be associated with Christ. Jesus, however, had a different opinion of John. After John was beheaded by Herod, Jesus said that among those born of women, there had not been a greater prophet than John the Baptist.[17] These are the words that the Saviour spoke concerning John.

And when it was time for Jesus to be baptized, Jesus sought John out, not the other way around. This happens in Saint Matthew 3:13-17. Let me recount it for you.

Jesus came from Nazareth, where he had been abiding with his earthly parents, Joseph and Mary. And when he approached John, John refused to baptize him, saying that he, John, needed to be baptized by Christ, and why should Christ come to him for baptism.

---

[17] Matthew 11:11.

Water Baptism

John knew that Jesus was the Holy One of God, and therefore had no sins to wash away. Jesus knew this too, but even so, he again instructed John to baptize him. By doing so, they would fulfil all righteousness. You see, John the Baptist and Christ Jesus were sent to this earth with a definite plan of salvation. Every detail of this plan had been decided before Jesus ever left the side of the Father in heaven. That is why Jesus said they would be fulfilling all righteousness when John baptized him, meaning that they would be fulfilling all the righteous details of the plan for human salvation.

When Jesus came to this earth, he took upon himself the form of sinful flesh, becoming as one of his people and thus having the same natural passions and desires as any normal person. When he came to John, he was ready to begin his ministry. Jesus did not need to go to him for baptism. Jesus did not need baptism for *himself*. He was not a sinful man. He came to be baptized so that *we* might see the example he was setting before us, and follow it.

Saint Matthew 3:16-17 tell us that after Jesus was baptized, he came up out of the water and the heavens opened to him. And the Spirit of God descended. And a voice could be heard saying, "This is my beloved Son, in whom I am well pleased."

God repeats this in Saint Matthew 17:5, "This is my beloved Son, in whom I am well pleased; hear ye him." What Jesus did and said while he was on this earth was but the will of the Father. Therefore, let us see in the following chapters what Jesus says to us about water baptism. Let us see if he tells us that we must be baptized before we can be saved.

Chapter 4

Nicodemus is Taught

In order that you, dear reader, get a better understanding of water baptism, I think it wise to tell you what it says in the scripture records concerning water baptism. I will begin by recounting Christ's words to Nicodemus in Saint John 3:1-8.

Nicodemus, a Pharisee, came to Jesus at nighttime. He was a man of authority, a ruler of the Jews.

The Pharisees, do you remember, were a Jewish sect merely pretending to be righteous. They were a people that practiced hypocrisy.

Nicodemus, even though he was associated with this Jewish sect, recognized that Jesus was a teacher from God. He had heard of, and perhaps had seen, Christ performing miracles. So he was convinced that God was with Jesus, for no man could do the miracles Christ was doing unless God was with him.

Jesus made no mention of the miracles that he had performed, but he did answer Nicodemus's unspoken question. You see, the Lord Jesus could perceive what was in a man's heart. And he knew what the unspoken question in Nicodemus's heart was. Nicodemus wanted to know the way to salvation. Jesus's answer was doubly emphatic. He said, "Verily, verily, I say unto thee, except a man be born again, he cannot see the kingdom of God."[18]

Nicodemus was confused. To experience a rebirth when one was of a mature age is humanly impossible. So Nicodemus asked how this could be, since it was impossible for a man to enter into his mother's womb a second time and be born again.

Jesus replied, "Verily, verily, I say unto thee, except a man be born of water and of the Spirit, he cannot enter into the kingdom of God."[19] There you have it, dear brothers and sisters. Jesus was not referring to a natural birth. Christ was meaning that we must experience a spiritual rebirth if we are to enter into the kingdom of God. We must first be born of water, then of the Spirit.

---

[18] John 3:3.
[19] John 3:5.

Water Baptism

Now, when we are born, we come out of that which has us surrounded and covered. Therefore, to be born of water means that we must be covered with water first, then come forth from the water. Thereby signifying that when we are covered by water, the old us passes away. And when we come up out of the water, we are a new person in Christ. We have been reborn in spirit. That is the answer that Christ gave to Nicodemus. If we expect to enter into the kingdom of God, we must submit ourselves to the ordinance of water baptism. There are no other ways to interpret the Lord Jesus's words.

The Saviour then said to Nicodemus that there was a difference between births. He said, "That which is born of the flesh is flesh; and that which is born of the Spirit is Spirit."[20] Nicodemus was mystified. To him these things were unheard of. Then the Saviour told Nicodemus that he, Nicodemus, needed to be born again and that it should not come as a surprise to him.

This generation in which we live is just as difficult to convince of these truths as the generation was in the days when Christ was living on this earth. People will try to find all sorts of excuses and explanations to escape the commands of our Saviour. When the Son

---

[20] John 3:6.

of God spoke those words to Nicodemus more than two *thousand* years ago, he was speaking to the *whole* world, to the people of every race, color, and creed. He was speaking to all future generations, as long as time shall last. Those things that Christ said to Nicodemus still bind us today. His words will not pass away.[21]

I am going to tell you now, dear reader, what happened after Jesus's encounter with Nicodemus. The following comes from Saint John 3:22-30.

Jesus and his disciples traveled to Judaea. Once there, they began baptizing and spreading Jesus's gospel, the one he had come to this earth to bring to humanity. John the Baptist was also baptizing at that time, but he was in Aenon near to Salim because of the abundance of water. The Jews who came to John the Baptist told him that all men came to Jesus and were baptized.[22]

John knew that it was only fitting and proper that all men should be drawn to the Saviour. He told those that brought him this information that he was sent before Christ, and that Christ would increase, but he would decrease.

---

[21] Matthew 24:35.
[22] The record tells us that Jesus did no baptizing himself, but that his disciples baptized those that accepted his gospel.

Water Baptism

John the Baptist's mission on earth was drawing to a close. But the gospel of the Lord Jesus would go on and on, spreading through the centuries to the uttermost parts of the earth. And of his kingdom there would be no end.

Chapter 5

Jesus Instructs His Disciples

After the Son of God had carried on his ministry here on this earth for approximately three years, he was betrayed by one of his disciples, Judas Iscariot, and handed over to sinful men who wanted his death. Each of the first four books of the New Testament gives an account of this betrayal. Each of these New Testament books also gives an account of the trial and crucifixion of the Saviour. One of the most complete records of these things is given in the book of Saint Mark. So it is Saint Mark that I will mostly recount for you here. I will also recount a few details from Saint Matthew, Saint John, and Saint Luke that are not in Saint Mark. I will begin by recounting for you an abridged version of Saint Mark 14:1-50.

The chief priests, scribes, and elders had sought, for a long time, a way to craftily destroy Jesus. So when Judas Iscariot came to them and desired to betray Christ to them, they were happy, and they promised Judas money for his betrayal. This occurred at the time of year when the Jewish people were preparing to celebrate the Passover with a feast.

Jesus ate the Passover feast with his disciples in the city of Jerusalem. And while they were eating, he said to them that one of them eating at the table would betray him. The disciples asked their Master one by one who it was that would do this thing, for the Saviour knew who it was that would betray him to his enemies. Jesus answered, "It is one of the twelve, that dippeth with me in the dish."[23]

After they had eaten the Passover feast, Jesus and his disciples left the house where they had eaten and crossed the brook Cedron[24] to the garden of Gethsemane. Jesus and his disciples often retired to this garden, and Judas Iscariot knew the place well. So on this night, he came to the garden with a company of men and officers from the high priests and Pharisees. Judas approached Jesus, hailing him as Master. Then Judas kissed him. This was a signal to those with

---

[23] Mark 14:20.
[24] John 18:1.

Judas that they were to take Jesus away, for he would be the Son of man.

Saint Matthew 27:1-10 tell us that after Judas Iscariot realized his actions would bring about Jesus's death, he went to the chief priests, scribes, and elders and gave them back the thirty pieces of silver that they had given him for betraying Christ to them. But the chief priests and scribes only brushed aside Judas's admission of the terrible wrong that he had done. His admission meant nothing to them, just as he meant nothing to them now that he had served their purpose. Let him make amends himself, they told him. Then Judas threw down the silver that they had bribed him with and went out and hanged himself. The chief priests and scribes took the money that they had bribed Judas Iscariot with and bought a burying ground to bury strangers in. It became known as "The field of blood,"[25] because it was purchased with blood money.

Saint Mark 15:1-15 and Saint Matthew 27:11-26 tell us that Jesus was tried before Pontius Pilate, the governor of Judaea at that time, who found no reason to condemn Jesus to death. The chief priests and scribes, however, produced false witnesses who testified that Christ was a blasphemer, one who made himself to be the Son

---

[25] Matthew 27:7-8.

of God. Many of the people who held high offices in those days looked on Christ as an impostor, and they continuously sought ways whereby they might do away with this Jesus of Nazareth. Their chance had come with Jesus's arrest.

When Pilate desired to release Jesus, the chief priests, scribes, and other high officials swayed the people to call for someone else to be released instead. There was a custom in those days that at the feast of the Passover the governor would release to the people any prisoner that they requested. So when Pilate asked the people if he should release Jesus to them, they, being beforehand instructed by the chief priests and elders, asked that Barabbas, a murderer and insurrectionist, be released to them. And they cried out in a loud voice to crucify Jesus. Pontius Pilate, after protesting at great length, released Barabbas to the people and delivered Jesus to be crucified, after Pilate had him whipped to please the people.

Saint John 19:1-15 give us a little more insight into why Pilate gave in to the people. You see, Pilate was a man afraid of public opinion. And he was anxious to please the chief priests, elders, and people. His governorship was under subjection to the Roman Empire, and the Jews had told Pilate that if he released Jesus, he was no friend of Julius Caesar, who was the Roman Superior. He would

Water Baptism

be no friend of Julius Caesar because he would be siding with Jesus, who had spoken against Caesar when Jesus called himself the king of the Jews. When Pilate asked the chief priests and people if he should have their king crucified, the chief priests grasped the opportunity to further denounce Christ. They answered Pilate, saying that they had no king but Caesar. The governor saw that he could not dissuade them from their purpose, and that is why he delivered Jesus to them to be crucified, even though he thought Jesus was innocent.

Saint Mark 15:27, Saint Matthew 27:38, Saint John 19:18, and Saint Luke 23:32-33 all mention that Jesus was crucified with two thieves. One on the right, and one on the left. Saint Luke[26] goes on to tell us that one of the thieves spoke to Jesus bitterly, saying, "If thou be Christ, save thyself and us."[27] But the other transgressor reproved him sharply, saying that they themselves were receiving their just rewards, but that Jesus had done no wrong. Then he turned to the Saviour and said, "Lord, remember me when thou comest into thy kingdom."[28] The eleventh hour had come for this man on the cross, and he felt an urgent need for security beyond the grave. And

---

[26] Luke 23:32-43.
[27] Luke 23:39.
[28] Luke 23:42.

the Lord Jesus answered the thief in the same understanding way that he had always shown to repentant sinners during his life on this earth. Jesus said to him, "Verily I say unto thee, today shalt thou be with me in paradise."[29] A wonderful sense of security must have filled the heart of that thief. He no longer had to dread the condemnation that had awaited him during judgment. His sins had been pardoned.

Now, there are those who will present Christ's promise to the thief as sufficient scriptural proof that we do *not* have to be baptized to obtain salvation. These same individuals may even reference the woman taken in adultery[30] to strengthen their argument against water baptism. They will say that Jesus did not tell the thief on the cross *or* the woman taken in adultery that they had to be baptized to be saved. That is very true. There is no biblical record of the Saviour

---

[29] Luke 23:43.

[30] Saint John 8:1-11. The story of the woman taken in adultery goes something like this: Jesus was teaching in the temple on the Mount of Olives when the scribes and Pharisees brought a woman to him. They had caught her in the act of committing adultery. They said, "Now in the Law Moses commanded us to stone such women; what then do You say?" It was a test you see. They wanted to disprove him. It took some minutes before Jesus answered. And when he did, he said, "He who is without sin among you, let him be the first to throw a stone at her." One by one all the scribes and Pharisees left, until it was just Jesus and the woman. Jesus looked at the woman and said, "Woman, where are they? Did no one condemn you?" She said, "No one, Lord." Then Jesus said, "I do not condemn you, either. Go. From now on sin no more."

telling these two people that they needed to be baptized. But let us look at it this way: Who is there to say that these two people had not already been baptized? Saint Luke 3:21 says the following: "Now when all the people were baptized, it came to pass, that Jesus also being baptized, and praying, the heaven was opened." The record tells us that "all the people" were baptized. The thief on the cross and the adulterous woman could have been among "all the people" who were baptized. Can anyone truthfully say otherwise?

To present Christ's promise to the crucified thief and Christ's words to the adulterous woman as scriptural proof that baptism is *not* essential to our salvation is unwise, because there is no scriptural backing to that effect. But we do have the words of Christ Jesus—on more than one occasion—telling us that we *must* be baptized to be saved, that we must be born again. Born of water, and of the Spirit.[31]

Jesus rose the third day after his crucifixion and burial, and he appeared to his disciples for forty days. During that time, he increased their understanding of the scripture and upbraided them

---

[31] John 3:5.

for their slowness in believing those things surrounding his resurrection.[32]

The records of Saint Mark, Saint Matthew, Saint Luke, and Saint John all tell us that Jesus's disciples repeatedly refused to believe those who had told them that they had seen Jesus alive again. These same disciples had seen him perform wondrous miracles that no ordinary human could possibly do. They had been present when Jesus had triumphantly entered Jerusalem riding on the ass and the Father had spoken from heaven at his request.[33] Three of the disciples had been with him on the mountain when Jesus had been transfigured. They had seen his face shine as the sun and his clothing shine as the light. They had seen Moses and Elias appear and talk to Jesus, and they had heard the voice of God speaking from a cloud, acknowledging Jesus as his son.[34] Yet after Jesus was crucified before their very eyes, they refused to believe that he had risen from the grave.

Saint John 20:24-29 tell us that Thomas, one of the twelve, refused to believe that Jesus had come back from beyond the grave. He needed proof before he would believe. He needed to see where

---

[32] Mark 16:1-18; Matthew 28:1-17; Luke 24:1-43; John 20:1-29.
[33] Mark 11:1-11; Matthew 21:1-11; Luke 19:28-40; John 12:12-19.
[34] Mark 9:1-13; Matthew 17:1-13; Luke 9:28-36.

Water Baptism

the nails had pierced Jesus's hands, put his finger into the prints to prove they were real, and thrust his hand into Jesus's side where it had been pierced. The Saviour appeared to the disciples when Thomas was present and thoroughly convinced Thomas that he was the same Jesus that Thomas had followed.

Saint Luke 24:50-53 tell us that Jesus then led his disciples outside the city to Bethany, a village about two miles east of Jerusalem. And there he gave them his final instructions, for he was going back to the Father. His work was finished on this earth, and he was leaving the carrying on of his gospel in the hands of the men who had been his disciples during his ministry. Saint Luke goes on to tell us that while Christ was giving his disciples his final blessings, he was separated from them and carried up into heaven.

Dear reader, let us look at these final instructions that the Lord Jesus gave his disciples. They are of infinite importance to you and me. We must believe and obey them. There are two scriptural records of Christ's final instructions to his disciples. The first is recorded in Saint Matthew 28:18-20. The other record of final instructions, which deals with water baptism, is found in Saint Mark 16:15-18.

In the record that Saint Matthew gives, Jesus tells his disciples, "All power is given unto me in heaven and in earth. Go ye therefore, and teach all nations, baptizing them in the name of the Father, and of the Son, and of the Holy Ghost."[35] Christ gives his last words with complete authority. He instructs his disciples to go forth and teach all nations the gospel of Christ. But is that *all* Jesus told his disciples to do? No, dear reader, that is most definitely not all he told them to do. He instructed his disciples to first, *teach* all nations. Then, after they had been taught the gospel, he instructed his disciples to *baptize* them in the name of the Father, Son, and Holy Ghost. Furthermore, Jesus instructed his disciples to teach all nations to observe *everything* that he had told his disciples. And, again, one of those things we are instructed to observe is baptism.

In the record that Saint Mark gives of Christ's final instructions to his disciples, we find much the same substance that is given in Saint Matthew's record. But in Saint Mark's record, Christ is *very* emphatic about baptism. In Saint Mark's record, the Lord Jesus says,

> Go ye into all the world, and preach the gospel to every creature. He that believeth and is baptized shall

---
[35] Matthew 28:18-19.

Water Baptism

be saved; but he that believeth not shall be damned. And these signs shall follow them that believe; in my name shall they cast out devils; they shall speak with new tongues; they shall take up serpents; and if they drink any deadly thing, it shall not hurt them; they shall lay hands on the sick, and they shall recover.[36]

These are the last words that the Saviour spoke to his disciples as they appear in Saint Mark's record. In this record, Jesus says that only those who believe *and* are baptized will be saved.

Those who argue against water baptism will contend that baptism has nothing whatsoever to do with their salvation. They will tell you that they are saved to be baptized, and not baptized to be saved. If they do get baptized, they will tell you it is simply an ancient, outdated custom that they are observing. That baptism does not really apply to us today. They ignore the fact that when Christ gave a command in his word, that command was everlasting.

I wish to raise this thought in your mind at this time: If we are saved to be baptized as some believe, instead of being baptized to be saved as the word of God says, then what is the use of being

---

[36] Mark 16:15-18.

baptized at all? If we are already saved, then it is just a waste of time and effort to bother being baptized. If baptism is an ancient, outdated custom, then it would have died out a long time ago. So why, then, do people still observe baptism today? Think about.

In the following chapters we will see if Christ's disciples preached and taught the gospel as he instructed them to do. And we will see whether they baptized those who accepted the gospel of Christ.

Chapter 6

Simon Peter's Sermon on the Day of Pentecost

Simon Peter was a fisherman before Jesus called him to be a disciple.[37] When we read the scriptural record of Peter, we find that he was an impulsive man, one given to bursting into speech without first stopping to consider what he was saying. Peter, despite his impulsiveness, was a man born to be a leader of men. Christ recognized this quality. That is why he told Peter "from henceforth thou shalt catch men."[38] Christ was telling Peter that he was to become a harvester of mankind, a harvester of human souls. But before Peter became the leader Christ knew he would be, Peter acted impulsively.

Saint Mark 14:27-72 tell us that the night Jesus was betrayed, the night the Lord's supper was instituted, Peter vowed to Jesus that

---

[37] Luke 5:1-11.
[38] Luke 5:10.

he would follow him anywhere, even into death. But Jesus knew what the future held. He knew the weakness of human flesh. And he told Peter that even in that same night, before the cock crowed twice, Peter would deny that he knew Jesus three times.

Judas Iscariot betrayed Jesus into the hands of his enemies later that night. As they were leading the Saviour away, Peter followed behind them. He even followed them into the palace of the high priest where they took Jesus. He sat with the servants and pretended to belong by warming himself by the fire. And that was the problem. He pretended to belong.

The servants confronted Peter three times that night; they were positive Peter was one of the men who followed Jesus of Nazareth. And each time Peter impulsively denied having any knowledge of Christ. The third time he denied the Saviour he cursed and swore. Then the cock crowed the second time, and Peter remembered what Jesus had told him. And he went out and wept bitterly.

Saint John 21:1-17 tell us that after Jesus was crucified, Peter and some of the other disciples went fishing in the sea of Tiberias, not knowing that Jesus had arisen. Peter, no doubt, was remembering how he had failed Jesus. That is why we find him turning back to his old occupation. That of a fisherman.

Water Baptism

Peter and the disciples fished all night with no success. When morning came, they returned to shore. And Jesus was standing there, waiting for them. He knew that they were returning empty-handed, and he addressed them as children, asking if they had any meat. And they answered none. Jesus told them to cast their net on the right side of the boat. They did. When they tried to draw the net to shore, they could not, for there were too many fish in the net. One hundred and fifty-three fish to be precise. They were large fish, but the net did not break.

When Jesus appeared to his disciples that morning, they did not recognize him at first. But when they beheld the multitude of fish that they had netted from a single cast of their net, as he had directed, they knew him to be the Lord. Whereupon, Simon Peter, who was naked, wrapped himself in his fisher's coat and jumped into the water to swim to shore. The others followed in the boat.

Once they had all reached the shore, they found that Jesus had a fire of coals waiting with fish cooking on it. The Saviour also had bread to eat. He invited them to come and dine. And when they had eaten, Jesus said to Simon Peter, "Simon, son of Jonas, lovest thou me more than these?" Peter answered, "Yea, Lord; thou knowest that I love thee." Then Jesus said Peter, "Feed my lambs."[39]

---

[39] All three lines of dialogue come from John 21:15.

Three times Christ asked Simon Peter that morning if he loved him. And three times Peter answered that he did. Each time when Peter answered Jesus that he loved him, Jesus would tell him to feed his "sheep." The Master knew that Peter was remembering his denial of the Christ Jesus on the night of his betrayal and imprisonment. He knew that Peter doubtless considered himself unworthy to be a disciple of Christ any longer. Jesus had foreseen that Peter would fall into this state of mind, and he had acted accordingly.

Saint Mark 16:1-7 tell us that Mary Magdalene, Mary the mother of James, and Salome went to the tomb where Jesus was laid after his crucifixion. When they entered the tomb, for the stone at the door had been rolled away, they beheld a young man dressed in white, sitting in the tomb on the right side. And they were afraid. This young man told them to not be afraid and that Jesus of Nazareth had risen and was gone. Then he said, "But go your way, tell his disciples and Peter that he goeth before you into Galilee: there shall ye see him, as he said unto you."[40]

From this young man's words we can see that Jesus knew Peter was no longer considering himself a disciple. The Lord Jesus was

---

[40] Mark 16:7.

Water Baptism

making sure that Peter heard of his resurrection and would know where to find him. And now this brings us back to Saint John 21:15-19, where we find Jesus asking Peter if he loved him more than his fishing comrades, more than he loved his old occupation as a fisherman. Jesus loved this impulsive, unlettered man, and he wanted Peter to feed the hungry souls of the world his gospel. He knew that Peter had impulsively denied him, so he was calling Simon Peter back, back to the great commission of the cross. He said to Peter, "Follow me."[41] Thereby telling Peter to go forth into the world and preach Christ's gospel.

From that time forward, Peter was a staunch, devout follower and minister of the gospel of Jesus Christ. In Acts 2:1-41, Peter delivers his first sermon to the people on the day of Pentecost. Right before Jesus had ascended, he instructed his disciples to remain in Jerusalem until they received the Holy Ghost. So on the day of Pentecost, they were all in one place when the Holy Ghost descended with the rush and roar of a tempest. The Holy Ghost took the form of cloven tongues that looked like fire and touched every one of them. Then the disciples began to speak in other tongues.

---

[41] John 21:19.

When the people heard the disciples speak to them in the languages in which each man was born and raised, they were amazed and confounded. Some even scoffed and mocked the disciples, saying that they were drunk on some new wine.

Peter heard these mocking accusations and immediately rose in defense of the wondrous works that the Holy Ghost was performing through the disciples. He said,[42] "For these are not drunken, as ye suppose, seeing it is but the third hour of the day. But this is that which was spoken by the prophet Joel.[43]"

Then Peter told them of the prophesy that Joel had made, concerning what they had seen and heard that day in Jerusalem. He then refreshed their minds concerning their recent condemnation and crucifixion of Jesus of Nazareth, a man who had performed miracles and wonders among them, whom God approved of. He continued by telling them that David had spoken of Christ Jesus and his resurrection. Peter then told the people of Jerusalem that this same Jesus, whom they all had known while he was living amongst them and whom they for spite and envy had condemned and put to death, had now been made by God the Father both Lord and Christ.

---

[42] Acts 2:15-16.

[43] Joel was an ancient Hebrew prophet. There is a book of his prophesies in the Old Testament.

Water Baptism

When the people of Jerusalem heard these words, they were pierced in their hearts, for they realized then what they had done. They had killed the Son of God.

Then they asked Peter and the rest of the apostles, this question: "Men and brethren, what shall we do?"[44] They were asking how they could become reconciled in the sight of God, how they could gain forgiveness for the terrible, sinful state they were in. Peter's answer points the way to salvation and puts into action the instructions that Jesus left with him and the other disciples before he ascended. Peter's answer is pertinent to each and every one of us.

"Repent, and be baptized every one of you in the name of Jesus Christ for the remission of sins, and ye shall receive the gift of the Holy Ghost."[45] That is the answer that Peter gave to them. And here we see the gospel of Christ in operation. The disciples were carrying on as Jesus had instructed them to do.

Dear reader, do not deceive yourself or go through this life with the mistaken thought that Peter's answer does not apply to you today. It is as binding on us today as it was on the people he gave his answer to more than two thousand years ago. Lord Jesus laid down

---

[44] Acts 2:37.
[45] Acts 2:38.

that plan of salvation for the whole world, for as long as time shall last.[46]

Peter expounded the gospel to the people of Jerusalem that day at great length. Pointing out to them that the promise of salvation was made to them, and their children, and all those that further encouraged them to save themselves from the stubborn, ungodly generation of that day.[47] The generation of that era was doubtless wicked and unchristian. When John the Baptist began his ministry, he called many of those that came to him for baptism "vipers."[48] And Christ called many of the people of the era hypocrites and unbelievers. Read the first four books of the New Testament and you will find many, many instances where he bitterly denounced them.

Acts 2:41-47 tell us approximately three thousand souls gladly received and believed the preaching of the gospel of Jesus Christ the day Peter gave his sermon, and all were baptized. And they all steadfastly followed the doctrine that the apostles had preached to them.

---

[46] John 12:48-50.
[47] Acts 2:39-40.
[48] Matthew 3:7.

Water Baptism

After that, Simon Peter was the spokesman for the disciples in almost every instance when they assembled together. He had indeed become a leader of the "sheep" of Christ. Filled with the Holy Ghost, he disregarded the warnings he received and threats of personal harm because of his preaching and teaching of the gospel of Jesus Christ. Peter would not be shaken in his stand for Christ again. He knew and acknowledged the one of whom he was preaching. He had been called by the Master for this work. He himself had experienced the wondrous mercy and forgiveness of the Saviour. He *knew* the hopeless state of all those that were still living in their sins, that knew not Jesus Christ as their Saviour. Peter, with the help of god, surmounted all obstacles and opposition, and steadfastly carried on the gospel of Christ. Truly, he had become a fisherman of men, of human souls, for Christ.

Simon Peter wrote two books of the New Testament: The First Epistle General of Peter and The Second Epistle General of Peter. In his first book, Peter makes a very binding statement concerning water baptism.[49] First, though, Peter brings to our remembrance the patience and longsuffering of God toward this sinful world. And he reminds us how eight souls were saved by water when Noah built

---

[49] 1 Peter 3:20-21.

his ark. Then Peter says that water baptism, in a like manner, "doth also now save us (not the putting away of the filth of the flesh, but the answer of a good conscience toward God)."[50] Meaning that through water baptism, we know that we are obeying the command that Christ left for us.

For did not Jesus say to Nicodemus, "Expect a man be born of water and of the Spirit, he cannot enter into the kingdom of God."[51] Peter was with Christ the night Nicodemus came to him. So he heard and remembered the answer that Christ gave to Nicodemus. And like the good servant of the Saviour that Peter was, he has passed this most vital ordinance on to future generations, telling us that water baptism is vital to our salvation.

---

[50] 1 Peter 3:21.
[51] John 3:5.

Chapter 7

Peter Baptizes Cornelius

In chapter three, I told you that being baptized with the Holy Ghost does not automatically exempt you from water baptism. And then I used Peter baptizing Cornelius as an example to illustrate that point. I want to recount for you, now, the full story of how Peter came to baptize Cornelius, because I cannot stress enough the importance of water baptism. So, in Acts 10:1-48, we find in Caesarea an Italian whose name was Cornelius.

As I already told you, Cornelius was a Gentile, and he was a devout man who feared God with all his household. He prayed to God always and gave much to the needy.

Do you remember what I said about Gentiles? Up until that time, the gospel had been preached almost exclusively to Jewish people, even though Jesus had instructed his disciples to go and "teach all nations,"[52] his gospel.

Well, Cornelius had a vision. And he had it about the ninth hour of the day, which in our present manner of reckoning the hours of the day would be about three o'clock in the afternoon. In his vision, he saw an angel of the Lord. And this angel told Cornelius that God approved of the good deeds he did for the poor and wanted him to send men to Joppa to ask for Simon Peter, who, when he came, would tell Cornelius what he must do to obtain salvation.

Immediately after the angel had departed, Cornelius called three of his trusted men before him and he told them of what had transpired. Then he sent them on the way to Joppa to bring back Simon Peter, who, from the beginning, was the recognized leader and spokesman for the disciples.

The next day, while the men from Cornelius neared Joppa, Simon Peter went up to the roof of the house he was staying in to pray. He did this about the sixth hour, which is noon by our present time. As he was up there, he became quite hungry. So while the people of the house were preparing food for him, Peter fell into a trance.

---

[52] Matthew 28:18-19.

Water Baptism

While Peter was in this dreamlike state, the heavens opened to him and a vessel shaped like a great sheet was lowered down by its four corners. And in this strange craft there were every manner of beast and fowl and creeping things that were on earth.

Then a voice from heaven told Peter to rise and slay the creatures in the sheet-like craft. And once slain, the voice told Peter to eat the creatures. But Peter argued with the voice of God from heaven, claiming that he had never eaten things that were unclean or common. Whereupon the Lord chastised Peter and told him that what he had cleansed, whatsoever it may be, was not common or unclean. Here we see Peter's impulsive manner predominating even his close association with God.

The voice of God told Peter three times to eat the contents of the sheet-like craft. Then the craft returned to heaven.

Peter knew that what he had seen and heard was a vision, and while he was meditating on what he had seen and heard that day, Cornelius's messengers arrived. And the Spirit of God informed Peter that three men were seeking him. The Spirit then instructed Peter to get down from the roof and go with the men without question. So Peter went down and met with the men Cornelius had sent. He asked them their reason for coming to him. They told Peter all that had happened. That they had come from Cornelius, who was a man of good report among all the Jews and who feared God. And that Cornelius had received a warning from God through his Holy angel to send for Peter and to hear the gospel that he would preach to them. When Peter heard this, he invited the men into the house and put them up for the night. The next day they departed for the house of Cornelius.

Their journey lasted two days. When Peter entered Cornelius's house, Cornelius fell at Peter's feet and began to worship him, believing Peter to be a personage from heaven. But Peter would not permit this. He knew himself for what he was, a simple fisherman who was spreading the gospel of Jesus Christ, and not in any sense a Godlike figure. Jesus had chosen him to gather souls for the Christ that died on Calvary's cross,[53] and not for men to look up to. Peter lifted Cornelius to his feet and told him that he was just a man, the same as he himself was, and not one to be worshipped.

Cornelius had called together his relatives and close friends so that they might hear those things that the angel of the Lord had said that Simon Peter would tell him. The first thing that Peter said to

---

[53] Luke 23:33. Calvary is the place where Jesus was crucified. In Mark 15:22, John 19:17, and Matthew 27:33, the place is called Golgotha, meaning "the place of a skull."

Water Baptism

them was that he was violating Jewish customs by coming into Cornelius's house. But then he told them that God had revealed to him that all men were the same in the sight of God. When he was thus enlightened, he immediately came with the men that Cornelius had sent. Peter desired to know why he had been sent for.

Whereupon Cornelius explained to him all that had come to pass. And when Peter had heard these things, he understood what the vision he had had on the roof in Joppa meant. Therefore he said to these people that he understood that God was not a "respecter of persons,"[54] that the Lord did not have any favorites among men. All those of *every* nation who lived righteously in the fear of God were acceptable to him. Peter had but to remember the parting instructions of the Master to know these things. He had heard Jesus command them to preach the gospel to all nations.[55] But Peter was a Jew, and he had been taught not to associate with those of another nationality. Now, though, he could see the meaning of this gospel that Christ had commissioned him to preach. The saving grace of God had been extended to include all men, of every nation, regardless of the race creed.

---

[54] Acts 10:34.
[55] Matthew 28:18-19.

Peter then preached to Cornelius and all those with him the gospel of Christ Jesus. He told them that through Christ Jesus all those who believed in him would have their sins forgiven. And while Peter was preaching, the Holy Ghost touched all those whom he was preaching to. When the brethren who had come with Peter from Joppa saw this, they were amazed. The Holy Ghost had fallen on the Gentiles.

What happened next is very important.

When Peter saw that the Holy Ghost had come upon these people, he asked those who had come with him from Joppa: "Can any man forbid water, that these should not be baptized, which have received the Holy Ghost as well as we?"[56] Then he commanded them to be baptized in the name of the Lord.

This is unshakable proof of the essentialness of water baptism, being visited by the Holy Ghost is not enough. Notice Peter's words: "Can any man forbid water . . . ?" I am asking that same question to all those who teach otherwise.

Can you withhold water to prevent someone from being baptized?

---

[56] Acts 10:47.

Water Baptism

The answer comes to us from the eternal words of God Almighty: "Except a man be born of water and of the Spirit, he cannot enter into the kingdom of God."[57]

Dear friend, these words give us absolutely no other course to take but to observe water baptism.

---

[57] John 3:5.

Chapter 8

Philip Preaches and Baptizes

Philip was one of the original twelve disciples that Jesus called. His home was in the city of Bethsaida. The same city where Simon Peter and his brother Andrew were from. Immediately after Philip was called, he led another man to Christ. This man's name was Nathanael, and he became one of the twelve disciples of Christ too.[58]

In Acts 8:5-40, we find this same Philip carrying on the gospel as Christ instructed the disciples to do. Shortly after Stephen was stoned to death for preaching Christ's gospel,[59] Philip traveled to the city of Samaria, and there he preached Christ to them. He brought great joy to the city of Samaria, healing many and casting out

---

[58] John 1:43-51.
[59] Acts 7:54-60.

unclean spirits. And the people heard and received the words that he spoke joyfully. Then when they believed Philip's preaching, concerning the kingdom of God and the name of Jesus Christ, they were baptized, both men and women.

Here again, we see one of the original twelve disciples carrying on with Christ's gospel, exactly as Christ instructed. Those people of Samaria did not question whether being baptized was essential to the salvation of their souls. They accepted the gospel as it was preached to them, and it was preached to them by a man who had been in very close association with Jesus Christ while he was here on earth. He had been chosen to do this very work by the Son of God.

At the time Philip was evangelizing the city of Samaria, a sorcerer named Simon was dwelling there. He had bewitched the people of this city, from the highest to the lowest, with sorcery. He had made them believe that he had "the great power of God."[60] And all the people esteemed him. But at the coming of Philip all this changed. The people recognized in him a true representative of Almighty God after beholding the miracles that he did. And they believed, and they were baptized.

---

[60] Acts 8:10.

Water Baptism

Simon the sorcerer also believed the gospel that was preached to him, and he too was baptized. Afterward, he traveled with Philip, watching all the miracles and signs that Philip performed. Simon wondered at what he beheld. It was a power far beyond the power his witchcraft gave him. It was a power far beyond God in heaven. And Simon coveted this power.

When the apostles that were in Jerusalem heard that the people of Samaria had accepted the word of God, they sent Simon Peter and John to the city. Now when Peter and John arrived in Samaria, they prayed that the people who had been converted might receive the Holy Ghost. Because, as yet, these people had not received the Holy Ghost. They had only been baptized in the name of the Lord Jesus. So Peter and John prayed, and they laid their hands on these new converts, and the new converts received the Holy Ghost.

Simon the sorcerer saw what the apostles did. The power they wielded was the kind of power he had always wanted. So he offered money to Peter and John, saying, "Give me also this power, that on whomsoever I lay hands, he may receive the Holy Ghost."[61]

Peter said to Simon the sorcerer, "Thy money perish with thee, because thou hast thought that the gift of God may be purchased

---

[61] Acts 8:19.

with money."[62] Then Peter told Simon that he had no part in the power that came from the Lord, because his heart was not right in the sight God.

Simon the sorcerer had believed the things that Philip had preached and had been baptized. But at his request for power, Peter had read what was still in his heart: bitterness. Peter told Simon that he was still a prisoner of wickedness, and unrighteousness, and evil. Doubtless Simon was remembering former days when, through the use of witchcraft, he was a person of high regard in Samaria. Now, if he was to be a follower of Christ—and he did confess to believe in him and he was baptized—those former things would never happen again. No more could he have people look on him in respect and fear. He would be just another man now, one who recognized his need of salvation and who had surrendered to the call of Christ, the Saviour of mankind.

Peter instructed Simon to repent of the wickedness that was in his heart and to pray to the Lord that the evil thoughts in his heart would be forgiven. Simon then requested that Peter and John pray to the Lord for him that he might not be visited with the wrath of God.

---

[62] Acts 8:20.

Water Baptism

Simon the former sorcerer had been made to see the evilness of his heart, and he had repented of it.

The scriptures[63] tell us that an angel of God instructed Philip to leave the city of Samaria, and to journey southward into the desert to Gaza. Philip did as he was bid. As he journeyed, he came upon an eunuch, who was the queen of Ethiopia's treasurer. The eunuch was sitting in his chariot, reading the prophet Esaias's words. He was reading the prophesy concerning the arrest of Christ Jesus, and of his silence before his accusers. The eunuch read the question the prophet asks out loud: "Who shall declare his generation? for his life is taken from the earth."[64]

The Spirit of God instructed Philip to go to the eunuch. And when he heard him read Esaias's words, he asked the eunuch if he understood what he was reading. The eunuch informed Philip that he could not understand the scripture he was reading, unless he had someone to explain it to him. Here was an opportunity for evangelism. This was what the Master had called Philip to do. Then, beginning with the scriptures that the eunuch was reading, Philip preached to him Jesus Christ. He told the eunuch of Christ's

---

[63] Acts 8:25-40.
[64] Acts 8:33.

conception, of his life, and of the wondrous miracles that he had performed. He told him that Jesus Christ was the Son of God, and that he had been born to become the Saviour of mankind. He told the eunuch of how Jesus had shed his blood on the cross in a place called Calvary[65] for the sins of mankind. That how, through his death, we might have life and have it more abundantly.

When Philip preached Jesus to the eunuch of Ethiopia, what else could he say? He told the eunuch that we must be baptized with water to obtain salvation through Jesus Christ our Lord.

You may ask, how do we know that Philip told the Ethiopian eunuch all these things? How do we know that he told him that we must be baptized with water to gain salvation?

Well, after Philip had preached Jesus Christ to the eunuch, they continued on their way in the chariot. And as they journeyed, they came upon some water. Now, dear reader, here is where we know that Philip told the eunuch all these things that I said he told him. When Philip and the eunuch came to this water, in this desert country through which they were traveling, the eunuch said to

---

[65] Luke 23:33. Again, Calvary is the place where Jesus was crucified. In Mark 15:22, John 19:17, and Matthew 27:33, the place is called Golgotha, meaning "the place of a skull."

Water Baptism

Philip, "See, here is water; what doth hinder me to be baptized?"[66] You can plainly see that Philip must have told the eunuch that he needed to be baptized with water to be acceptable to our Lord and Saviour Jesus Christ. If Philip had not told these things to him, why did the eunuch request to be baptized when they came to the water?

Born of water, and of the Spirit.[67] And so it will remain, until the end of time. People may try to explain water baptism out of Christ's plan for human redemption, but they are only deceiving themselves. He put it in his plan for you and me, and unless we accept his plan the way he set it up, we most definitely will not be acceptable to him.

When the eunuch made his request to be baptized, Philip told him that if he believed with all his heart the things that he had preached about Jesus and Jesus's plan for human redemption, he could be baptized. Then the eunuch answered, "I believe that Jesus Christ is the Son of God."[68] That is what Philip wanted to hear him say. That he believed that Christ was the promised Saviour that would redeem mankind. And the eunuch did believe it. He commanded the chariot to stop. Then he and Philip left the chariot

---

[66] Acts 8:36.
[67] John 3:5.
[68] Acts 8:37.

and walked into the water, and Philip baptized him. Baptized him with water. Can anyone say otherwise?

After the eunuch had been baptized and they had come up out of the water, the Spirit of God took Philip away. Then the eunuch continued on his homeward journey, filled with gladness because he was a new creature in Christ Jesus. He had been born again of water and of the Spirit of God.

Philip showed up again in Azotus, where he continued on, preaching the word of God in every city until he came to Caesarea.

If you but read the book of Acts in the New Testament, you will find that the disciples left no stone unturned for those they could preach Christ's gospel to, uncaring of the deadly peril their very lives were in as they did so. They just went on and on. As the Master said to them, "Go ye therefore, and teach all nations."[69] And go they did, and teach they did. And when their teaching was accepted, they baptized those that were converted to Christ.

---

[69] Matthew 28:19.

Chapter 9

Paul is Converted and Baptized

The man who would later become the Apostle Paul was first introduced in the New Testament as Saul. He was born and reared in Tarsus, a city of South Turkey near the Mediterranean Sea. Tarsus was, at that time, an important seaport on the river Cydnus. Saul was instructed from his early childhood by one of the most learned men of the day. This man's name was Gamaliel.[70] This teacher of Saul's was a Pharisee, nevertheless he was a doctor of the law[71] and a man of good reputation among the entire populace.

Saul was taught the old law of the fathers. The Mosaic Law. And he was zealous toward this biblical law of his fathers, even to the consenting of putting to death the disciples who were preaching to

---

[70] Acts 22:3.
[71] Acts 5:34.

the people Christ's gospel,[72] which is referred to first in Acts as the new way. Meaning that this new doctrine that was being preached was a new way of faith in God. A new way of salvation based on the teachings of Jesus of Nazareth, who died on a cross outside Jerusalem.

But this new faith was unknown to many. So the disciples were often driven out of cities because of their preaching this new doctrine. In the case of Stephen, a devout young evangelist, he was stoned to death.[73] Acts 8:1-3 tell us that Saul was present when Stephen was stoned to death, and he supported this murderous deed. He believed that Stephen and those like him were preaching a false way of salvation to the people. They were false prophets in Saul's eyes, and he believed they should be dealt with as such. He entered into every house and imprisoned all those that were converts to this new faith, both men and women. Then Saul caused wide and general destruction and devastation to the early church that the apostles had established. But his efforts only resulted in a more widespread evangelizing of the gospel of Christ.

In Acts 9:1-18, Saul threatens the disciples with death if they continued to teach and preach in the name of Jesus of Nazareth. But

---

[72] Acts 22:3.
[73] Acts 7:54-60.

Water Baptism

then he decided to do more than threaten. He decided to have himself vested with authority from the high priest of Jerusalem. He wanted letters from the high priest telling those in authority in the synagogues at Damascus that if he should find any believers of this new way of faith, either men or women, he had the authority to bring them as prisoners back to Jerusalem. Saul was sincere in his persecution of the followers of Christ. He believed that these people were deceiving themselves and those that they had converted to this new way of faith.

And so with a company of men Saul journeyed toward Damascus. As he drew high to the city, he was suddenly engulfed in a light from heaven. This light was brighter than the noonday sun, and it blinded Saul. He fell to the ground. Then a voice said to him, "Saul, Saul, why persecutest thou me?"[74] This was the voice of Jesus speaking to him out of the heavens, asking him why he had been persecuting his followers and devastating the church that Jesus himself had died to establish.

But Saul knew not who it was that spoke to him. He answered the voice, "Who art thou, Lord?"[75] And the Lord answered him, "I

---

[74] Acts 9:4.
[75] Acts 9:5.

am Jesus whom thou persecutest."[76] Saul began to tremble; he was much amazed. And he realized then what he had been doing. He saw how terribly wrong he had been, giving his consent to the brutal slayings and imprisonments of those teaching the gospel of Jesus. Saul asked the Lord Jesus, "What wilt thou have me to do?"[77] He wanted, zealously, to serve God the right way, and the Lord Jesus knew this. So Jesus told Saul to rise and go into Damascus. And there he would be told what he must do.

When Saul rose from the earth, he could not see. His eyesight was gone. Those that were with him led him by the hand into the city of Damascus. His entry into the city was very different from what he had planned it to be. He had journeyed to Damascus prepared to make prisoners of any and all that he found preaching this new way of faith. But instead Saul was the prisoner, a prisoner of Jesus Christ.[78] Saul was blind for three days. During that time, he neither ate nor drank anything. And he stayed at the house of Judas, who lived on Straight Street.

There lived in Damascus at that time a disciple whose name was Ananias, and the Lord appeared to him in a vision, saying,

---

[76] Acts 9:5.

[77] Acts 9:6.

[78] Saul (Paul, then) refers to himself as a "prisoner" in Philemon 1:1.

Water Baptism

"Ananias."[79] He answered and said, "Behold, I am here, Lord."[80] Then the Lord told Ananias to go to Straight Street to the house of Judas to ask for Saul of Tarsus. And the Lord told Ananias that Saul was currently praying, and in his prayers he had seen a vision of Ananias coming to him and restoring his sight when Ananias placed his hand on him. But Ananias was afraid to go near Saul. He had heard of this man's reputation for persecuting the saints of the Lord in Jerusalem. And Ananias knew that Saul had come to Damascus to continue his work of persecution, having authority from the local chief priests for this very thing. It is understandable that Ananias would feel this way about Saul, especially after everything he had heard about the man.

But the Lord Jesus put Ananias's fears concerning Saul to rest. He told Ananias that Saul was a chosen messenger, that he would bear the name of Jesus Christ to the Gentiles, and kings, and the children of Israel. And that he, Jesus Christ, would show Saul what great things he must suffer for this work that he would have to do for Christ. So Ananias rose and went to Saul, and he placed his hands on him. He said to Saul, "Brother Saul, the Lord, even Jesus,

---

[79] Acts 9:10.
[80] Acts 9:10.

that appeared unto thee in the way as thou camest, hath sent me, that thou mightest receive thy sight, and be filled with the Holy Ghost."[81]

Imagine the joy and thanksgiving that Saul must have felt in his heart at Ananias's words. Jesus, whom he had persecuted, had granted him forgiveness. The Lord Jesus was giving him back his sight and extending to him the Holy Ghost. Ananias had accepted him as a brother. In the years that followed, Saul never ceased to be humbly grateful for the mercy and pardon that he was granted that day in Damascus. More than once, in his future letters to the brethren, he refers to himself as one who was the chief of sinners, a persecutor of the saints.[82]

Immediately after Ananias had placed his hands on Saul and spoke to him as he did, the blindness left Saul's eyes. Then Saul rose and he was baptized.

There are those who may tell you that the apostle Paul (no longer Saul), in his letter to the Ephesian brethren, teaches that baptism is unessential to salvation. In Ephesians 2:8-9, Paul says, "For by grace are ye saved through faith; and that not of yourselves: it is the gift of God: Not of works, lest any man should boast." In

---

[81] Acts 9:17.
[82] 1 Timothy 1:12-17.

these two verses, Paul is not casting aside water baptism as something that is no longer needful. He is speaking of the grace of God, telling us that through our faith in this saving grace we obtain salvation, that we must trust and obey the commands that Jesus Christ left for us, that we cannot hope to gain the crown of life by works only. That through our faith in God's graciousness, and through our observance of his mandates, lies our salvation.

Yes, there are certain verses in the New Testament that may seem like Paul is teaching that baptism is unessential in Christ's plan for human redemption. But let me ask you this: Why did Paul submit to baptism in Damascus if it was of no importance? Why, too, did Paul go on to baptize others if being baptized with water is unnecessary?

I want to remind you that this man, Saul of Tarsus, later Paul, was a very well-educated person. He was taught by Gamaliel, a doctor of the old Mosaic Law, a law that was given to Moses by the Lord Almighty on Mount Sinai. He knew all the rules and regulations of this law of his fathers, and he zealously followed these rules and regulations to the point that he imprisoned and even consented to the putting to death of those that taught otherwise.

Therefore, would it not be but characteristic of Paul to acquaint himself perfectly with all the mandates of this new way of salvation that Jesus Christ had established?

Yes, and that is exactly what he did.

Acts 9:19-31 tell us that immediately after Saul had regained his strength from the three harrowing days where he did not eat or drink while he was sightless, he joined the disciples that were there in Damascus and began to preach the gospel of Christ in the Jewish synagogues. He preached that Jesus of Nazareth was the Son of God, proving to them that Christ was indeed the Messiah that the Jewish forefathers had prophesied would come.

Those that heard Saul were amazed, and they wondered at his sudden about-face. After all, he was the same man who had imprisoned and consented to put to death those who had called on the name of Jesus in Jerusalem, and he had come to Damascus to continue his work against those who taught this new belief.

The Jews of Damascus were furious, and they deliberated together to kill him. But Saul found out about this conspiracy. So while the Jews watched the gates of the city, the disciples lowered Saul down the wall in a basket at nighttime to escape.

Water Baptism

When Saul returned to Jerusalem, he was a man with an entirely different attitude toward this new way of salvation that was being preached in the land. He had left Jerusalem bent on annihilating this new doctrine, but was returning a believer and an upholder of the very thing that he had set forth to destroy. Unfortunately, the disciples who were in Jerusalem would have nothing to do with him. They were still afraid of him, and they did not believe that he was a disciple of Christ Jesus. They believed his conversion was a trick to further his campaign of persecution and disruption.

But Barnabas spoke on behalf of Saul, and he told the other disciples that Jesus had intercepted Saul on his way to Damascus and that Jesus had chosen Saul to preach his gospel to the Gentiles, kings, and Israelites. After hearing this, the other disciples accepted Saul as one of them. Saul stayed with the disciples then and preached the gospel in and around Jerusalem. And he disputed with the Greeks until they endeavored to kill him. When the other disciples found out, they sent Saul back to his home in Tarsus by way of Caesarea.

Acts 13 and 14 tell us that Saul remained in Tarsus for a considerable amount of time. Then Barnabas came to Tarsus seeking him, and the two went on many missionary journeys together. Many of which ended with Saul and Barnabas running for their lives. I am not going to talk about those journeys in this book. I mention them only so you can see how fervently Saul preached Christ's gospel, even at the expense of his own life.

I want to turn your attention, now, to Saul's plea in Acts 22:1-16. In his plea, Saul recounts how the Lord stopped him on his way to Damascus and took his sight. Then Saul tells those listening what Ananias instructed him to do. Ananias said, "For thou shalt be his witness unto all men of what thou hast seen and heard. And now why tarriest thou? arise, and be baptized, and wash away thy sins, calling on the name of the Lord."[83] He told Saul to waste no time about being baptized. Salvation is that way. We have no assurance of time. Christ says that today is the day of salvation, now is the accepted time. And there was no hesitation on Saul's part. He immediately obeyed the instructions that Ananias gave him: He rose and was baptized.[84] Can any person now say that in his writings Saul teaches against baptism's essentialness?

---

[83] Acts 22:15-16.
[84] Acts 9:18; Acts 22:16.

Chapter 10

Paul Preaches and Baptizes

Paul traveled a lot, preaching the gospel of Christ. In almost every city that he preached in, there were those who accepted the salvation that he preached, but there were also those who did not believe and sought to kill him. And when this could not be accomplished, they stirred up the people against Paul. In Lystra, a city of Lycaonia, the Jews prevailed so strongly on the people's feelings that the people stoned Paul and dragged him out of the city, leaving him for dead.[85] Do you suppose Paul remembered Stephen[86] as he fell, bruised and battered, under the stones that were hurled at him?

Eventually, a vision sent Paul and Silas to Macedonia. That portion of Paul's missionary work is what I am going to talk about

---

[85] Acts 14:8-20.
[86] Acts 7:54-60.

in this chapter. In Acts 16:9-34, the vision Paul had was of a man from Macedonia standing before him. The man said, "Come over into Macedonia, and help us."[87]

So Paul and Silas, and those that were with them on their missionary tour, straightaway left for Macedonia. And after resting in two other cities, they finally arrived in Philippi, which was the greatest metropolis of that part of Macedonia. They stayed in the city of Philippi until the first Sabbath after their arrival. Then they journeyed outside Philippi to a place where people prayed by a river side. They sat down and began talking to the women who came to this place of prayer.

One of these women was named Lydia, and she was a cloth saleslady. She worshipped God, and when she listened to the gospel that Paul and his party were preaching, the Lord opened her heart so that she accepted the things that these evangelists were saying. Then she, and all those of her household, were baptized. Afterward, she insisted that Paul and Silas and the rest of their party stay in her house. But only if they felt that she was faithful to God. They did feel she was faithful, so they stayed.

---

[87] Acts 16:9.

Water Baptism

Now, there was in the city of Philippi a maiden that practiced divination, and those that were in authority over her gained much by this maiden's predictions. This same maiden followed Paul and those that were with him for several days, and as she followed them, she shouted that they were servants of God Almighty and that they would show the people of Philippi the way to redemption. Eventually Paul became weary of this. So he turned to her and said, "I command thee in the name of Jesus Christ to come out of her."[88] And the spirit of divination left her.

When those who had profited from this maiden's predictions found out that their source of income was no more, they laid hold of Paul and Silas and brought them before the magistrates, claiming that they were teaching things that were subversive to their customs and that were unlawful for them to observe according to their Roman upbringing. The people rose up against them then, and the magistrates tore the clothes off of Paul and Silas and commanded that they be beaten. After the people had beaten them, they cast them into prison.

---

[88] Acts 16:18.

The keeper of the jail was charged with keeping Paul and Silas from escaping, so to be doubly sure they could not, he put them in an inner cell and fastened their feet in stocks.

Here is a wonderful manifestation of faith. They had been stripped of their clothes and whipped until their naked backs were a mass of welts. Then they were cast into prison. And to further add to their miseries, their feet were fastened in stocks, which made it impossible for them to move about, or even stand. Yet Paul and Silas were not dismayed. Those that were imprisoned in the same jail heard them praying and singing at midnight. They still praised God, regardless of the hardships and privations that they were enduring carrying on the gospel. How many evangelists today would preach the gospel under such persecution? The number would be small indeed.

While Paul and Silas were praying and singing, there was a great earthquake. And the very foundations of the prison were shaken. The doors on all the cells opened, and every prisoner's fetters were loosened. The jailer woke up and saw what had happened. He drew his sword to take his life, thinking that he had let all the prisoners escape. Then Paul, seeing what the jailer was about to do, called out to him and told him not to harm himself, for none of the prisoners

Water Baptism

had escaped. When the jail keeper heard this, he asked for a light. Then he rushed into the disciples' cell and fell, trembling, at the feet of Paul and Silas. When he regained his feet, he brought them forth from the jail and he asked them what he must do to be saved.

This jail keeper realized that these men were indeed servants of the most High God. Here was proof positive that they had been preaching the truth. Now this man wanted to know what he must do to obtain salvation. Paul and Silas told him that he should believe in the Lord Jesus Christ, and he would be saved, so too would his household. Then these evangelists preached the gospel of Christ to the jailer and to all those that were in his household. The jailer then took Paul and Silas, that same hour of the night, and washed the welts on their backs. In turn, Paul and Silas baptized the jailer and his household at once.

Now, there is something I would like to draw your attention to. There are many who use the answer that Paul and Silas gave to the jailer as scriptural evidence that belief alone in Jesus Christ[89] is sufficient to obtain salvation.

I have written to publishers of religious tracts asking them to have the writers of the material that they publish explain this

---

[89] Acts 16:31.

statement more fully. I have asked that they explain *why* Paul and Silas baptized the jailer and his household if belief alone is sufficient. But I have not received any replies, for the very obvious reason that there is no answer that they could give without admitting that being baptized with water is a definite and important part of Christ's plan for our redemption. And that is what the manmade creed, which they are expounding, forbids them to do. They will tell you that someone said that the Bible teaches we have to be baptized to be saved, and then they will hasten to say that baptism has nothing whatsoever to do with our salvation. They will point out verses like Acts 16:31, which says, "Believe on the Lord Jesus Christ, and thou shalt be saved," and others of like content as proof of scriptural backing to substantiate their claim.

Dear reader, that is how many are being deceived and misled. They are being told only part of Christ's plan for our salvation. We must believe in Jesus before he can save us. That is an established fact. But if we are looking to Christ Jesus for redemption from our sins, we must do the things that he left for us to do. Remember what Christ said to Nicodemus? Remember what Christ said to his disciples before his ascension? Rest assured, he meant those words. We have no choice but to be baptized.

Water Baptism

The condemnation of hell awaits all those who teach only part of Christ's plan for human redemption. They will be classed as false prophets in the Judgement, because they have misled human souls by their misrepresentation of the scriptures. They will be guilty of taking away from God's word. Read the last three chapters of the book of Revelation and see what it says about those who mislead and take away. There is a terrible punishment in store for all such people.

After the jailer and his household were baptized, the jailer invited Paul and Silas into his home, and he gave them meat, all the while rejoicing and believing in the Lord. And all those of his house believed too.

I can furnish undisputable scriptural proof that the Apostle Paul baptized those who next received the gospel. I have only to turn to the book of Acts in the New Testament and read about this man of Tarsus to know this. Paul and Silas baptized those at Philippi,[90] and Paul also baptized disciples in the name of the Lord Jesus in Ephesus.[91] Do not delude yourself into thinking that one method of salvation was preached in one city, while another plan was preached

---

[90] Acts 16:9-34.
[91] Acts 18:18-21.

in another city. The same plan of salvation was preached to all. Christ laid down his life on the cross to establish this one plan of human redemption for all nations, as long as time shall last. And every part of that plan, which he perfected, is just the same today as it was more than two thousand years ago when his disciples began preaching and teaching it after Christ ascended back to the Father.

Paul continued his missionary work for many years, and he traveled to many strange countries and cities that were far from the scenes of his childhood. And he endured much persecution and privation. Nevertheless, he steadfastly carried on, bringing the message of Jesus to those that knew him not. It is believed he was martyred in Rome during the reign of Nero, which was about the year AD 61.[92]

---

[92] 2 Timothy 4:1-8.

Chapter 11

The Conclusion

In the preceding chapters, I have set forth the biblical history of water baptism. I have shown how it was introduced by John the Baptist, and how Jesus followed in John's footsteps carrying on where John left off. I have furnished undeniable scriptural proof—proving to all who care to read the Bible themselves—that Jesus commands us all to be baptized. That baptism is a definite part of Jesus's plan for our salvation. Can there now be any question in your heart as to the absolute necessity of being baptized to obtain salvation?

Let me ask this question to all who still contend otherwise: If, after you have read from the Holy word of God where Christ has commanded us to be baptized, you shove it aside as unessential, do you honestly believe in your heart that Christ will say to you on

Judgement Day, "Well done, thou good and faithful servant"? Can you honestly hope for such a greeting, if, while here on this earth, you scoffed at part of his plan for human redemption?

Dear friend, take God's word as Jesus gave it to us. By doing so, you will be far wiser than some on Judgment Day. All those who have based their hope of salvation on faith only would do well to remember that we are under command by the Lord Jesus to observe water baptism. But before we can be baptized, we must first commit deeds, or works, that would be worthy of repentance and baptism. Do you remember John saying that in chapter three?

What kinds of deeds, or works, must we do to earn baptism? Read on to find out.

In 1 Corinthians 13:1-13, the Apostle Paul tells us that charity in this life is greater in the sight of God than faith of hope. Charity means Christian love for our fellowmen in this life. Charity means helping those in need and those who are suffering. Charity means showing leniency to those who we would judge. Paul says that we could have enough faith to move mountains, but without charity, it avails us nothing in the sight of the Lord. Even if we turn over all our worldly possessions for the relief of the poor and give our bodies to be burned, we are still nothing in the sight of God without charity. So the Apostle Paul did not base his hope of eternal life on faith only. He steadfastly looked to Christ Jesus to guide the way he lived his life.

In 2 Timothy 4:7, Paul says, "I have fought a good fight, I have finished my course, I have kept the faith." Paul is saying that he has waged a successful fight against the forces of evil. He has lived a life that will bring him a crown of righteousness on Judgment Day. And when Paul says that he has finished his "course," he means that he has finished the work that Christ gave him to do.

Dear friend, I do not wish to weary you with constant reminders that we must base our hope of eternal life on faith and works combined, and not on faith only. The reminders I have given I give with the hope that you will realize the grim and awful consequences that await those who neglect this great salvation that he has given to us.

Let us look to the General Epistle of Saint James to further substantiate the fact that we have works to go with our faith. In James 2:14-26, James tells us that "faith without works is dead." He asks the question: Can faith alone save us? And then he answers: Faith alone profits us nothing. Read his words in the New Testament.

Do not delude yourself with the belief that on Judgment Day you are going to be judged by standards other than those that are laid down in the New Testament. That is the rule book that we are going to be weighed and measured by.

Dear friend, in closing, I do not want you to forget what Christ said to Nicodemus. Never forget those words. You will pay dearly for your forgetfulness if you do. "Verily, verily, I say unto thee, except a man be born of water and of the Spirit, he cannot enter into the kingdom of God."[93]

May the Grace of our Lord and Saviour Jesus Christ abide with one and all, both now and evermore. Amen.

---

[93] John 3:5.

1979 - Janice and Harold, his first dance.

1972- Giving Janice away at her wedding.

Early 1950's-Jane and Harold

Fall 1969 – Nancy, Janice, and Harold at the park.

Harold H Milton

January 16, 1990 – Janice and Harold on her birthday.

1980 – Janice and Harold.

Janice and Harold on Easter.

Janice reviewing Harold's books for publishing.

June, 1986 – Nursing graduation.

Harold's birthday.

Harold at the fireplace in their Bay Village home.

Janice with Harold on his birthday.

Fall, 1969-Jane and Harold.

Harold's grandparents, Alfred Farley and Lucinda Miller Farley.

House on W. 19th – Cleveland, Ohio.

Harold and dog, Heidi.

Harold's birthday.

1995 – Harold with great-grandaughter, Madison.

Harold and Madison.

Harold and daughter, Nancy.

Orville Blanton
with Baseball

Orville Blanton

1980s-Harold and Janice in the woods.

1993 -Harold gets his GED.

1994 – Harold in Vegas.

Jane and Harold after Nancy's death.

Harold with his GED.

www.ingramcontent.com/pod-product-compliance
Lightning Source LLC
Chambersburg PA
CBHW032301150426
43195CB00008BA/529